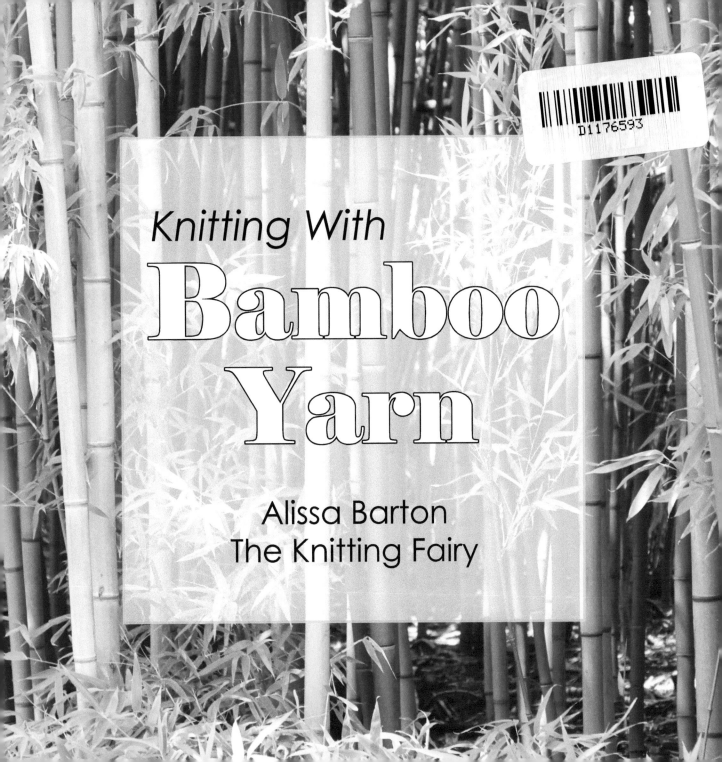

Knitting With
Bamboo Yarn

Alissa Barton
The Knitting Fairy

Knitting With Bamboo Yarn
Alissa Barton, The Knitting Fairy

Published by
Alissa Barton
2580 W. Camp Wisdom Ste 100 #247
Grand Prairie, TX 75052
http://KnittingFairy.com

First Printing

Theodora's Pearls yarns are available in fine yarn shops nation-wide. For stockists or to become one contact theodoraspearls.com

Facebook: http://facebook.com/knittingfairy
Twitter: @knittingfairy
Instagram: @theknittingfairy

Photography by Brad Barton http://bradbarton.us

Models:
Alex Moore - http://alexmooreactor.com
Mei Elizabeth - Instagram: @GorePrincessMei

Introduction

Several years ago I was introduced to a local Texas dyer by the name of Jennifer Miller. Jennifer is the owner and dyer behind Theodora's Pearls. Even though we lived in different parts of Texas, we hit it off right away. (with her wonderful sense of humor and gentle kindness, it's hard to not like Jennifer!) She began with bringing and then sending trunk shows of her amazing wool based yarns to my shop. Her work is just as engaging as she is and the trunk shows went very well. I even brought Jennifer and her yarns with me to sell in my booth at fiber shows. One such fiber show, DFW FiberFest, is where lightening struck. Jennifer met David and Michele at FiberLady. They introduced her to their bamboo yarns and just like that- BOOM! Magic happened.

Jennifer's beautiful colors came to LIFE on the bamboo. It's shimmery and silky, it has depth and dimension. Holding a skein of bamboo you feel compelled to work with it. But, what? That's where I came in. I knitted with it. I made shawls, scarves, sweaters. I wore it! I loved it, and in working with it I began to understand its limits and strengths. Bamboo yarns are magical, but they are not your average yarn. Do yourself a favor and do not knit socks with 100% bamboo. Cables are ok, but sparingly (it gets heavy fast!). Lace? It loves lace. Texture? Yes, please! Colorwork? A tad is fine, too much and you are into that weight issue again.

This book is the first release of what we hope will be many where I explore the strengths of working with bamboo yarns, its origins, and its place in our knitting world - because something this magical begs to be.

Table of Contents

Thank You for
believing in Fairies!
Alissa

The Story of Bamboo

For me, when I think bamboo the first thing that comes to mind are those "Lucky Bamboo" in containers and adorable Panda bears, laying on their backs munching away. Yarn? Never could I have imagined knitting with bamboo.

It turns out that those "Lucky Bamboo" aren't bamboo at all, rather they are a completely unrelated plant and a member of the Lily family. And, that bamboo-only diet that Pandas love is partially responsible for their population decline. What about the yarn? How did that happen?

Bamboo is a grass with over 1400 species and various grades of usefulness to us humans. Some species grow VERY rapidly, as fast as 36" (about a meter) in 24 hours, more typically bamboo grows between 1-4" a day. Still, 1-4 INCHES? Good grief! Talk to a gardener about bamboo and watch them get heated up. "Bamboo will take over everything! Don't plant it. Keep it in pots, throw it out." Even my sister, the world's most gentle gardener, had to resort to herbicide to fight back her neighbor's invasive bamboo patch that was threatening her beautiful yard. This rapid growth also makes bamboo quite the asset. The larger varieties are used as building materials, in some vulnerable places it is possible to have an entire home made of bamboo which is earthquake and cyclone resistant. Bamboo has been used to make anything from rafts to cookware to clothing throughout our history.

Yarn requires certain characteristics to make it desirable and traditional methods of making yarn from plant fibers such as retting flax to get linen result in stiff, twine like string. Hardly something you would want to drape over your body.

Enter modern technology. Today it is possible to break raw materials down in to their component pieces, gather the proteins out of this process and then reassemble them into something completely different. This makes our beautiful bamboo yarn a "man-made" fiber. It is strong, drapey, shiny, silky and the perfect yarn for warm weather wear. In fact, bamboo is taking over the textile market in general. Bamboo sheets, towels, t-shirts are everywhere. There are entire STOREFRONTS dedicated to all things made from bamboo. Bamboo fabrics are purported to be "anti-microbial, moisture wicking, anti-bacterial and biodegrade". All this while being more environmentally sustainable than other man-made fibers because it does not use wood and does not contribute to world-wide deforestation. Of course, like all man-made fibers, bamboo does have an environmental impact. Balancing the effects and benefits is a line we must all walk and Bamboo rayon is easier on our planet than other types of rayon available today.

Since I began knitting with bamboo I have come to appreciate it more and more each time. I find bamboo to be much like cotton in terms of the way the yarn behaves as it passes over my needles. It does not stretch or give and I prefer to knit bamboo on metal needles so that it slides easily. The finished garment drapes effortlessly around your shoulders or neck. Depending on what you make, it can stretch in length if it is a large garment, but you can help counteract this behavior by making sweaters with seams to hold its shape. I wash my bamboo pieces in the washer on delicate in a mesh bag and lay them flat to dry. Like any rayon fiber you should NOT leave it sitting damp in the washer or creases will form that take a while to remove. While this may seem to make bamboo finicky, I find that to not be true. Any hand-knitted item deserves proper care. You have dedicated hours, days, weeks, months of your life to create this piece and you should take the time to care for it properly so that you can enjoy your efforts for years to come.

Hua Mei

Hua Mei was the first Giant Panda cub born in the US to survive to adulthood

Finished size: 10 1/2" by 60" long

Materials Needed:
1 skein Auxonometer (Shown in Emerald)
US #6 (4.00mm) needle (any style)

Gauge: Approximately 6.5 sts/ in in lace.

Loosely cast on 69 sts.
Row 1: S1pwyb, (P1, K1, P1, YO, K2tog) 13 times, end P1, K1, P1.

Repeat row 1 until scarf measures 60" long, or length desired.
Bind off in pattern as follows:
S1pwyb, (P1, BO1, K1, BO1, P1, BO1, K1, BO1, K1, BO1), end P1, BO1, K1, BO1, P1, BO1. Break yarn, finish off.

Pro Tips:
Add or subtract stitches in multiples of 5.
The rib stitches hold the scarf flat, making blocking optional.
Buy 2 skeins and cast on 121 sts to make a shawl that is approximately 60"

Xiao Li Wu

Xiao Li Wu is a Giant Panda born in 2012 at the San Diego Zoo. His name means "Little Gift."

Finished size: 9" deep by 60" around

Materials Needed:
2 skeins Auxonometer (Shown in Blue Sky and Sand)
US #6 (4.00mm) 32" circular needle
Stitch marker.

Gauge: 5 sts = 1" in pattern stitch.

With Blue Sky, loosely cast on 300 sts. Place marker for Beginning of Row (BOR), Join to work in rounds.
Rnd 1: Purl. Do not break yarns throughout the piece.
Rnd 2: Join in Sand, Knit.
Rnd 3: With Sand, Purl.
Rnd 4: With Blue sky, Knit.
Rnd 5: With Blue sky, Purl.
Rnd 6: With Sand, (K2, S3pwyb) repeat around.
Rnd 7: With Sand, (P2, S3pwyb) repeat around.
Rnd 8: With Blue Sky, Knit.
Rnd 9: With Blue Sky, Purl.
Rnd 10: With Sand, Knit.
Rnd 11: With Sand, Purl.
Rnd 12: With Blue Sky, Knit.
Rnd 13: With Blue Sky, Purl.
Rnd 14: With Sand, S1pwyb, (K2, S3pwyb) repeat around to last 4 sts, end K2, S2pwyb.

Rnd 15: With Sand, S1pwyb, (P2, S3pwyb) repeat around to last 4 sts, end P2, S2pwyb.
Rnd 16: With Blue Sky, Knit.
Rnd 17: With Blue Sky, Purl.
Rnd 18: With Sand, Knit.
Rnd 19: With Sand, Purl.
Rnd 20: With Blue Sky, Knit.
Rnd 21: With Blue Sky, Purl.
Rnd 22: With Sand, S2pwyb, (K2, S3pwyb) repeat around to last 3 sts, end K2, S1pwyb.
Rnd 23: With Sand, S2pwyb, (P2, S3pwyb) repeat around to last 3 sts, end P2, S1pwyb.
Rnd 24: With Blue Sky, Knit.
Rnd 25: With Blue Sky, Purl.
Rnd 26: With Sand, Knit.
Rnd 27: With Sand, Purl.
Rnd 28: With Blue Sky, Knit.
Rnd 29: With Blue Sky, Purl.
Rnd 30: With Sand, (S3pwyb, K2) around.
Rnd 31: With Sand, (S3pwyb, P2) around.
Rnd 32: With Blue Sky, Knit.
Rnd 33: With Blue Sky, Purl.
Rnd 34: With Sand, Knit.
Rnd 35: With Sand, Purl.
Rnd 36: With Blue Sky, Knit.
Rnd 37: With Blue Sky, Purl.

Repeat rounds 6-37 twice more and then work rounds 6-21 once.

Bind off loosely in Blue Sky.

Xiao Li Wu

Pro Tips

For a 32" cowl you would cast on 160 sts. For a 48" cowl you would cast on 240 sts.

You can stop at any garter stitch section, just make sure you have worked 6 rounds of garter first.

When slipping stitches, be sure you do not pull the working yarn tightly behind the work. You want those stitches to lay flat, not to bubble up,

I used a regular bind off for this cowl, flexible bind offs tend to grow out of control with bamboo. Just be careful to match the circumference of the bind off to the circumference of the cast on.

Take a Tea Break

Knitters and tea seem to have a natural affinity. Curling up in front of a warm fire, a beautiful knitted project in your hands and a steaming mug of tea beside you are many knitter's ideal get-away.

Green tea is less appreciated by many, yet it has so many amazing health benefits - it contains many nutrients and antioxidants and there are boat-loads of studies out there if you want to read more. Yet, I find most people in America today tell me that they don't care for green tea. Because I do enjoy it, I will often ask why. I am told that they feel it is bitter, grassy or tasteless. Simply put, my friends, you are making your tea wrong!

The first step in enjoying a nice cup of green tea is to choose wisely. The cheaper-tea bag variety of green tea is a lesser grade and does not contain the best parts of the plant. While you can go crazy and spend ridiculous amounts of money on green tea, it is not necessary. The internet and specialty markets make laying your hands on premium green tea easy. Some can be found in pre-assembled tea bags, but I would encourage you to try loose tea. I put mine in filter bags (again, easy to obtain in the same kind of stores that sell loose tea) if I want something quick and easy, or I use an infuser-filter if I want to be able to steep the same leaves again and again. The variety of green teas available may seem staggering, so just jump in and grab one that seems appealing. I like Jasmine Pearls (little tiny balls of tea leaves, scented with jasmine flowers that are rolled together and dried. Just 7-9 little balls will make a cup of tea easily) or a nice needle leaf tea. The different varieties are all made from the same variety of plant, but processed differently and flavored with other plants.

Once you have chosen a tea to try, your next step is to heat the water. True tea lovers can wax poetic about the various temperature stages of boiling water. Different varieties of tea require different temperatures. For this, grab a sauce pan and add fresh water to it. Put it on the stove on a high heat and watch.

Shrimp-eyes (tiniest bubbles are just starting to form on the bottom of the pan) means that your water is around 160 degrees and perfect for delicate teas such as sencha and gyokuros.

Crab-eyes are slightly larger and there are just the first tendrils of steam starting to form. This water is approximately 175 degrees and is perfect for Chinese green teas, green oolong and white teas.

Fish-eyes are even larger yet and you will have steady steam. This water is now about 180 degrees and perfect for hardier green teas such as Gunpowder and Bai Mu Dan.

Green teas should not be made with water that has reached a rolling boil.

Of course, you could just get a thermometer, but watching the water is relaxing in its own right.

The last component to making the perfect cup of green tea is the length of time you leave the leaves in the water. 1-3 minutes is ideal and the general rule of thumb is the smaller the leaf, the less time you steep. Remove your tea leaves from the water by pouring it into a warmed cup (just fill it with hot tap water and let it warm while the tea steeps) or by pulling your infuser out of the water. Leaving the leaves in the water is what leads to bitterness, so don't do it.

You can re-steep your leaves several times in the same day. With each steeping the flavor will change subtlety. Toss your leaves when the flavor isn't pleasing or at the end of your knitting session.

Finally, don't add your spent leaves to the trash. Instead, let them dry out and add them to your garden soil or houseplants. They will add nutrients to the soil that your plants will love.

Bao Bao

Bao Bao is a Giant Panda born at the National Zoo in Washington D.C. in 2013. Her name means "treasure."

Finished size: 9" deep by 55" around
Materials Needed:
1 skein Auxonometer (Shown in Strawberry)
US #6 (4.00mm) 32" circular needle
14 locking stitch markers.
1 unique marker for beginning of round.

Gauge: approx 4.65 sts / inch over lace pattern.
Loosely cast on 225 sts, join to work in rounds.
Rnd 1: Place BOR marker. Purl.
Rnd 2: (YO, SSK, K1) around.
Rnds 3-6: Repeat rounds 1 and 2 twice.
Rnd 7: Purl.
Rnd 8: (SSK, K1, YO, SSK, K3, YO, SSK, K5, YO, [M]) around.
Repeat just round 8 for 7".
Work rounds 1-7 once more. Bind off loosely.

Pro Tips:
Change the circumference of your cowl by casting on more or less stitches in multiples of 15. Cowls that are bigger around will be less than 7" in the lace pattern. Be sure to allow yourself enough yarn to complete the garter lace border.
Round stitch markers tend to creep over and under yarn overs. You can help the situation by using the locking markers as ring markers. Just close them and put them on your needles. When moving the marker from the left to the right, keep the "lock" part of the marker on the opposite from the working yarn. So, when on a knit round, keep all those locks toward you.

Su Lin

Su Lin is a Giant Panda born at the San Diego zoo in 2005. Her name means "beautiful jade."

Finished size: 8" wide by 60" long

Materials Needed:
1 skein Auxonometer (Shown in Lipstick)
US #6 (4.00mm) needle (any style)

Gauge: Approximately 6.8 sts /inch in pattern stitch

Loosely cast on 68 sts.
Row 1: (RS) S1pwyb, SSK, (P1, K1) across to last 3 sts, P1, Kfb, P1.
Row 2: (WS) S1pwyb, (K1, P1) across to last st, P1.

Pro Tips:
Mark beginning of the right side rows with a removable marker or piece of contrasting yarn. If you do this you can tell at a glance by the position of the marker if you are on row 1 or row 2. Move the marker up as you work, try to keep it within 6" of your needles.

Change the width of your scarf by adding or removing stitches in multiples of 2 sts. Remember - a wider scarf will be shorter, a narrow scarf can be much longer.

The combination of knits and purls will keep your scarf flat.

Find Creative Ways to Wear Your Scarf

Tag Us with Yours #knittingfairybamboo

Terms and Abbreviations

K1 = Knit.

P1 = Purl.

S1(2, 3)pwyb = Slip the indicated number of stitches purlwise with the yarn held in back.

K2tog = Knit the next 2 stitches together.

SSK = Slip one as if to knit, Slip a second stitch as if to knit, insert the left needle tip back into the front of these two stitches (together), wrap the yarn around the right needle and knit these two stitches together through the back loops.

Kfb = Knit into the front and the back of this stitch. 1 stitch increased.

(RS) = Right side.

(WS) = Wrong side.

BOR = Beginning of round.

[M] = Marker.

YO = Yarn Over.

BO = Bind off

Alissa Barton
Knitting Fairy Original Designs

Alissa's more than 40 years of knitting experience began as a child. She quickly learned that she is "constitutionally unable to follow a pattern" and began modifying adult sweaters to something closer to her own size. From there it was a short jump to just writing the thing her own way from the beginning. She self-publishes her patterns as Knitting Fairy. The patterns have been published in a variety of publications and are available world wide through Ravelry.

Alissa travels and teaches classes at guilds, workshops, retreats and stores all around the US and Mexico since 1990.

You can follow her adventures on Ravelry, Facebook and Twitter as KnittingFairy and as TheKnittingFairy on Instagram.

Web: KnittingFairy.com
Facebook: KnittingFairy
Ravelry: KnittingFairy
Twitter: @knittingfairy
Instagram: @theknittingfairy

For teaching and workshop scheduling:
817-247-9210

KnittingFairy

To receive your eBook version, visit:
www.ravelry.com/redeem/alissa-barton-designs
And enter this code:

CPSIA information can be obtained
at www.ICGtesting.com
Printed in the USA
BVHW02n1343120918
527216BV00001B/3/P